CHAMBER CONCERTO IN D, RV 93

FOR VIOLA AND PIANO

Antonio Vivaldi

Arranged by
Lynne Latham

PIANO

This famous concerto, originally for lute, seemed the perfect fit for solo viola with a few minor adjustments. In the key of D Major and in 3 short movements, this work will delight audiences and gives the director a chance to highlight an outstanding violist without being overly technically taxing. Can be played all in 1st position, although some shifting may be preferred to execute trills. Also, an opportunity for a solo cello to play continuo.

keisersouthernmusic.com

CHAMBER CONCERTO in D, RV 93

I.

Antonio Vivaldi
Arranged by Lynne Latham (ASCAP)

4

II.

6

III.

SU835

8

Viola

3

SU835

Digital and photographic copying of this publication is illegal.

4

Viola

II.

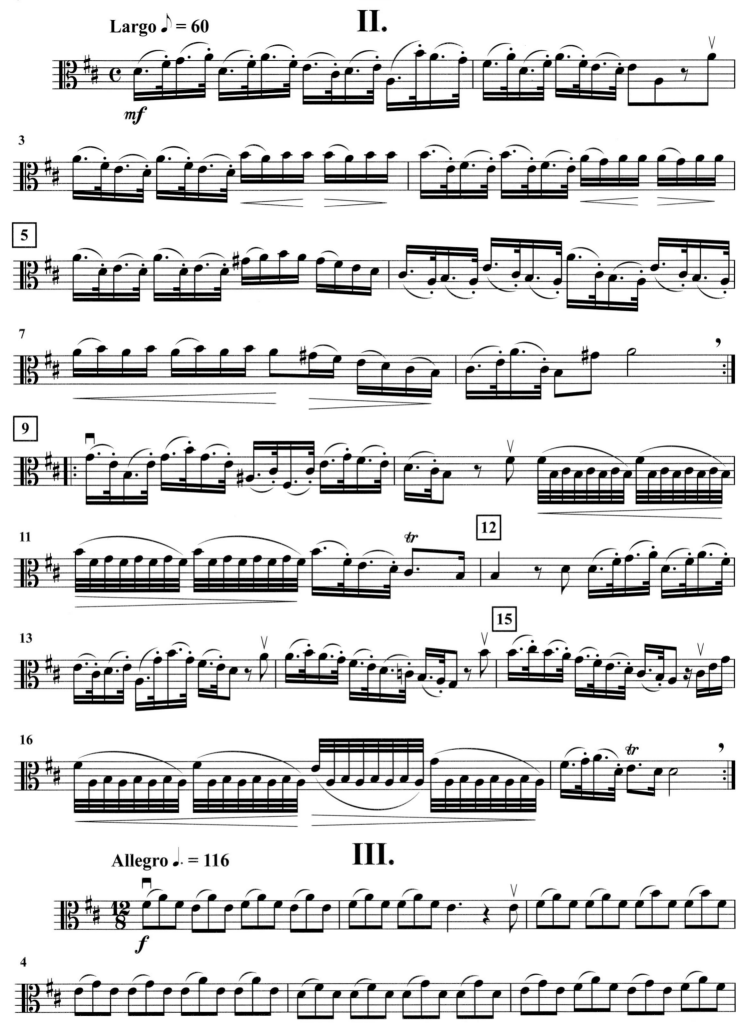

III.

Viola

CHAMBER CONCERTO in D, RV 93

I.

Antonio Vivaldi
Arranged by Lynne Latham (ASCAP)

SU835